Only one of Me

A love letter from Dad

Written by Lisa Wells, Michelle Robinson   Illustrated by Tim Budgen

GRAFFEG

There's only one dad quite like me.

I wish that there were two.
I'd have more time to spend
And I would spend it all with you.

There's only one dad quite like me.
I wish that there were three.

We'd journey far together –
Oh, the places we would see!

There's only one dad quite like me.
I wish there could be four.
I'd wrap my arms around you,
Keep you safe for ever more.

There's only one dad quite like me.
I'd sooner there were five.
I'd tell you how I love you
Every day I were alive.

But there is only one of me.
There aren't as many days
As I would want to spend with you,
In all those special ways...

To share the happy times with you,
To wipe away your tears,
To hold your hand and guide you
Through the weeks and months and years.

To tell you, *"I am proud of you."*

To teach you, *"You are strong."*

To let you know,
"I'll love you

Even after I am gone."

So I am asking Mummy
And I'm asking Auntie too,
Uncles, Grannies, Grandpas, friends –

Here's what you *all* must do:

Become a *little bit* like me –
Not *quite* like Dad, but try.

Help my children learn to live
If one day I should die.

Give my child your time and love.

Lead them far and wide.

Keep them safe and hold them tight
Long after I have died.

They say that time will help you heal.
I say, *I'll* help you, too.

It's *me* who'll be behind the crowd of people helping *you*.

That is what I'm asking *them*.
I'll ask *you* something, too.
It's just a little something
That I'm certain you can do.

Don't worry if you
cry a lot.

It's okay to get mad.

Even laughing's good –

There's more than one way to feel sad.

And be a little bit like Dad.

Be kind!

Be brave!

Be free!

Remember all the fun we had

When you remember me.

Love you always,
Daddy xxx

Lisa Wells

Lisa Wells was diagnosed with terminal bowel and liver cancer in December 2017. Determined to leave a legacy of love for five-year-old Ava-Lily and ten-month-old Saffia, she created Lisa's Army UK – a team of loved ones who will help support her husband Dan and the girls in a future Lisa won't live to see. Lisa has raised over £83k for charity and won Hello! Magazine's Star Mum Award. *Only One of Me* began as Lisa's love letter to her daughters. She hopes its publication will bring comfort to your family too. lisasarmy.co.uk

Michelle Robinson

Michelle Robinson lives a few streets away from co-author Lisa in Frome, Somerset. Michelle's dad was diagnosed with bowel cancer in 2016.

Meeting and working with Lisa has been the highlight of Michelle's career to date – even topping the time Tim Peake read her book *Goodnight Spaceman* to Earth from space. Michelle's many other books include *Ten Fat Sausages*, *How To Wash a Woolly Mammoth* and *Tooth Fairy In Training*. michellerobinson.co.uk

Tim Budgen

Tim Budgen lives on the sunny island of Hayling with his wife Julia, pet dog Baxter and Alfie the cat. His mum overcame cancer of the bowel and lungs in 2011. Tim has been a professional illustrator since 2016 after 18 years of teaching. He has produced work for Little Tiger Press, Hachette books, Maverick Publishing, ABRSM and Random House US. timbudgen.com

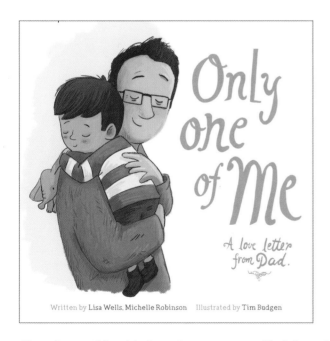

Only one of Me

A love letter from Dad.

Written by **Lisa Wells, Michelle Robinson**   Illustrated by **Tim Budgen**

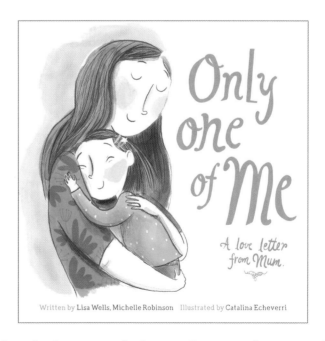

Only one of Me

A love letter from Mum.

Written by **Lisa Wells, Michelle Robinson**   Illustrated by **Catalina Echeverri**

Copies of both books are available at bookshops and also onlyoneofme.co.uk